Bernd Burkart Wilhelm Knobloch

# The World of the Dinosaurs

Dear Reader

You can use this press-out and play book in three different ways. By popping-out and glueing together all the pre-cut figures and stands from *The World of the Dinosaurs* you can very quickly assemble model dinosaurs to play with. Small areas of white card are attached to many of the figures to make them more stable. These are meant to be left on the figure, but if youdo not want them then cut them off carefully.

Besides this, you will find suggestions in the first few pages about how to make more figures, plants and scenery. If you like, you can make your own dinosaur game. You will also find information about the various types of paper and their uses and, just in case, advice about how to repair them. We were sure that you would want to know something about how dinosaurs lived, so we have included a lot of information on pages 3-8. You can test what you have learnt at the end with our quiz!

Since you will have to remove most of the pages from this book, we suggest that you keep the information pages in a folder. Then you will be able to refer back to them for facts more easily. You could even add more information about dinosaurs and build up your own reference file.



The Lutterworth Press
Cambridge

# Directions for assembly

## All about paper

Paper and cardboard are not something you should automatically throw away. They should be valued and appreciated. They are made of basic resources like wood or cellulose. Recycling paper is not exactly cheap either, as the recycling process uses a lot of water.

If you treat paper properly it can last a long time. You can see this in the case of very old books. Cardboard packaging can always be reused, as can wrapping paper if it isn't ripped. So you should treat paper carefully. If you do accidentally rip one of the playing figures in this book or some other piece of paper then you can repair it by applying adhesive tape to the back of the figure. If the tear is very large then you should reinforce the whole figure by sticking thin card on to the back of it. After the glue has dried you can cut away the excess card from around the edges of the figure.

It is best not to put drinks on the same table as paper since glasses can be knocked over very easily and paper absorbs liquid immediately. (Sugar from lemonade and other drinks makes stains as well.) But if an accident does happen, then you will just have to try to save as much as possible. Dab the cardboard figure carefully with absorbent paper like kitchen towels or blotting paper. Then lay the figure inside several layers of blotting paper between books. But make sure you don't get the books damp! You will have to replace the blotting paper with new pieces once it has become damp.

There are various sorts of paper and card:

We have already mentioned absorbent paper. This includes paper tissues, toilet paper and paper table napkins. Packing paper, coloured paper and wrapping paper are much stiffer and stronger. Card and cardboard are even stiffer and less likely to bend. The figures in this book are made of card. If you want to make more dinosaurs or landscapes and scenery then you should use card.

Corrugated cardboard is used to make packing cartons and boxes and is very strong. Corrugated paper is used for padding and could be useful to you. You could paint it to make it look like the sea.

Smaller boxes are often made of grey card. Book covers, folders and the back of pads of paper are made of thicker grey card. This helps protect writing paper from creases and folds.

Greaseproof paper and waxed paper resist fat and dampness, and for this reason they are often used to line clothes drawers.

Drawing paper and watercolour paper must be absorbent so that they can absorb watercolour paints.

Paper has *tensile* strength, which means that you can bend it and put pressure on it. This allows paper chains, paper darts, origami figures and also the figures in this book to keep their shape. Perhaps you have already noticed that paper rips more easily in one direction than in another. This is because it has a *grain* (the fibres all run in one direction). Try it out with various sorts of paper. You might want to rip out a lake or a hilly landscape and paint it.

You can paint on paper as long as it isn't waxed or greased or sticky. Use watercolour paints only on drawing paper or thick card. Other sorts of paper will become wrinkly or floppy. You can colour these other sorts of paper with felt-tip pens, coloured pencils or ballpoint pens. Wax crayons aren't so good because the colours smudge very easily.

The card in this book is printed on one side only, as all the figures have stands attached to the back to make them able to stand up.

## Stands

To make the figures stand on their own, the stands have to be attached to the figures and the landscapes so that they all tilt backwards slightly. If they do not, they will fall over. You will find pre-cut stands for each figure. Fold the ends to form a Z and glue one end to the base of the figure and one end to the body.

If you are making your own figures, you can work out the length of stand you need by measuring the vertical height of the figure (for example, of a Triceratops) from the shoulder to the fold of the base and adding about 4cm for the surfaces to be glued. Cut a strip of card the right length and draw lines across it 2cm from each end. Score along these lines with a fingernail, bend them to form a Z and then attach them to the figure.

A landscape or a skyscape will need two Z-shaped stands and a wide base.

## Scenes

To make a skyscape you will need a carton large enough to cut a piece of card of at least A3 size (approx. 42 x 30cm). Remember to include a wide base and leave enough card for stands. Then paint or draw the sky on the card.

**1. Fold the base towards the back**

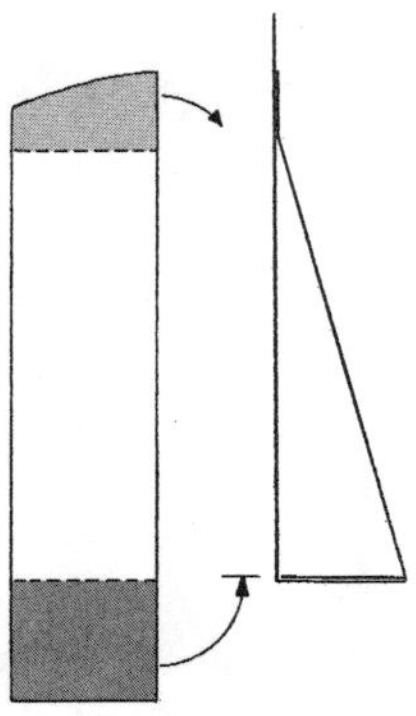

**2. Fold the lower end towards the back and the upper end towards the front. On the right is the side view of the figure with its stand attached.**

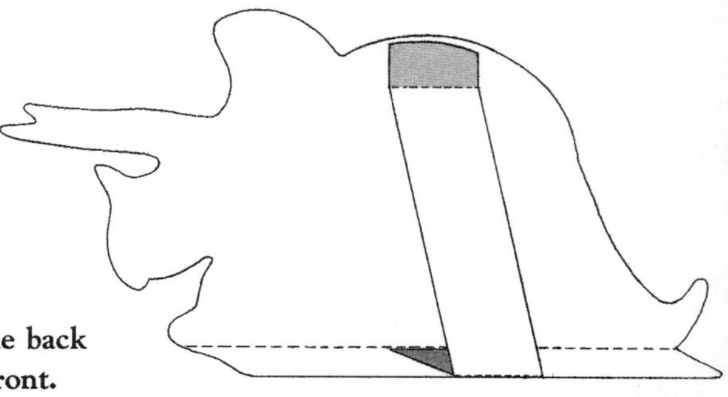

**3. Rear view of a figure with its stand attached.**

## Puzzle

Inside the cover of this book you will find a Stegosaurus skeleton which has already been divided up into squares. Cut around the squares as carefully as you can. It is easier to cut them out if you first divide the card in half. Afterwards try to piece them together again. Now you know what archaeologists have to do when they find bones and have to work out how the bones fit together!

## More suggestions

If you want to make additional dinosaurs or plants then it is best to draw them on drawing paper first, not forgetting the bases. Then cut out the figure together with its base, stick it on card and cut along the edges of the figure. Draw a line with a pencil and ruler on the back of the figure along where the base begins. Score along this line with a fingernail so that you can bend the base back more easily. You will find directions for making additional dinosaurs on pages 6-8.

You can make lakes and rivers with cellophane. This looks especially good if you draw a blue background with stones and water plants and a surrounding bank to go under it. Alternatively you could cut out a paper lake or river and paint that.

Corrugated paper is good for making the sea. The sort of corrugated paper you find in biscuit packets, which is reinforced on one side only or not at all, can easily be folded or rolled. You could use that sort to make a mountain landscape.

Flat landscapes can be drawn or painted on drawing paper, or cut out of crepe paper.

## Dinosaur game

You can make your own dinosaur game. Cut at least 20 playing cards out of thin card (from a shoe box, for example). They should be about 5.5cm square. You might like to ask someone to help you measure and cut the cards.

Take two cards and draw the same animal or plant on each, or stick matching pictures on to them. Repeat this, drawing (or sticking) a different animal or plant on each pair of cards. To play the game, turn all the cards picture down and mix them up. Each player in turn picks up two cards and shows the pictures. If a player picks up a pair then she or he takes it. The player with the most pairs wins. You can play this game alone. Older children could time you. How long does it take you to collect all the pairs? Write it down and see if you can do it faster next time. This way you can play against yourself.

Don't worry so much about going fast or winning that you forget to enjoy yourself. Games are supposed to be fun!

# How Dinosaurs lived

You have almost certainly already heard the word 'dinosaur' and may well have seen pictures of them. Perhaps you have even visited a natural history museum and seen a dinosaur skeleton. So you probably already know that dinosaurs, pterosaurs and ichthyosaurs lived millions of years ago and became about 65 million years ago.

Perhaps you have wondered how we know such a lot about dinosaurs and can even draw pictures of them, even though no-one has ever seen a living one. There have always been people who were interested in finding out about what the world was like before they themselves were alive. Some people have always wanted to know what the earth looked like before humans existed.

This is what happened about 300 years ago.

## The first dinosaur bones

The first recorded finding of a dinosaur bone was in 1676. A curious Englishman dug it up and took it to a scientist, the Revd Dr Robert Plot, to find out what animal it came from.

The state of scientific knowledge at that time meant that Dr Plot believed the bone belonged to a human giant. In fact, up until the beginning of last century people believed that the bones of large extinct animals were the remains of mythical creatures like dragons, unicorns and giants. Such bones often disappeared into private collections, never to be seen again.

We know that Dr Plot was looking at a dinosaur bone because he got someone to draw a picture of it. This picture has survived, and modern scientists can identify the bone as the knee end of a thigh bone of a Megalosaurus. Megalosaurus was a predatory dinosaur of the Mesozoic age.

If you look at pictures of dragons in books of fairy tales you will see that some pictures do indeed look like dinosaurs.

Dinosaur research didn't begin until over 150 years later. Then, in 1840, the Englishman Sir Richard Owen began to examine the huge bones that were being dug out of rock layers from the Mesozoic age.

Richard Owen rightly believed that the fossilized sections of skeleton were extinct relatives of the modern lizard. For that reason he gave these animals the name 'dinosaur', which means 'terrible lizard'. Thus, Richard Owen classified dinosaurs as reptiles.

## Mammals, reptiles, dinosaurs

Mammals are animals which bear their young live and feed them with milk. Mammals, including humans, and also birds (which are not mammals), maintain their body temperature through their blood circulation. They usually protect themselves from cold with their fur or feathers, and thus they are not constrained by heat and cold, and can move around quickly at any time.

Reptiles like lizards, snakes, tortoises and crocodiles lay eggs, which are hatched through the warmth of the sun. These animals draw heat from the sun to maintain their body temperature and their mobility. This means that their movement is restricted by the time of the day and the temperature.

Dinosaurs are classified as reptiles even though they did not crawl, but ran properly on two or four legs. For a long time scientists believed that dinosaurs' mobility was dependent on the sun only, as with all other reptiles.

But for several decades many researchers have been claiming that dinosaurs created some of their own body warmth. Today scientists are still arguing about whether dinosaurs were able to store solar heat (heat from the sun) in their massive bodies, or whether they produced their own body heat like mammals, humans and birds. Small dinosaurs would not have been able to store solar heat and must have produced their own. The scales of some small predatory dinosaurs developed into warm feathers. These animals were the ancestors of birds.

As well as the dinosaurs which lived on land there were crocodiles and ichthyosaurs, which lived in the water, and pterosaurs, which could fly. They were all reptiles.

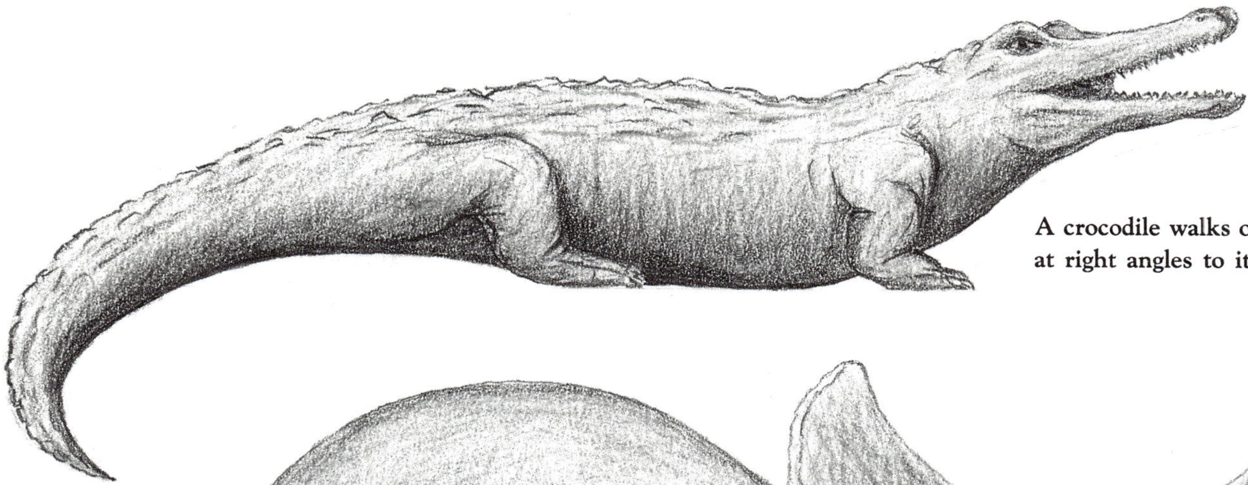

A crocodile walks on legs turned out at right angles to its body.

Triceratops stood like a mammal and ran on four legs.

Velociraptor belonged to the group of dinosaurs that ran on two legs.

## What was the world like?

Dinosaurs lived in the Mesozoic age, which began about 245 million years ago and ended about 65 million years ago. It is divided into the Triassic, Jurassic and Cretaceous Periods.

The question of where dinosaurs lived cannot always be answered exactly by saying, for example, in America or in Europe. First you have to look at what the earth was like in the Mesozoic age.

Up until the Jurassic Period all the continents were joined by land bridges. This meant that the dinosaurs could wander from one land area to another. Everything lay closer to the equator then. There were few mountains and the area of sea was much bigger than the land area. Because of this the climate was warm, damp, and without seasonal variation. These were ideal living conditions for dinosaurs.

Growing on land were various plants like tree ferns, conifers similar to our firs, and, in damp areas, tall equisetum (a type of horsetail). The ground was covered with shorter equisetum, ferns and lycopods (a type of clubmoss). There were no grass and meadows.

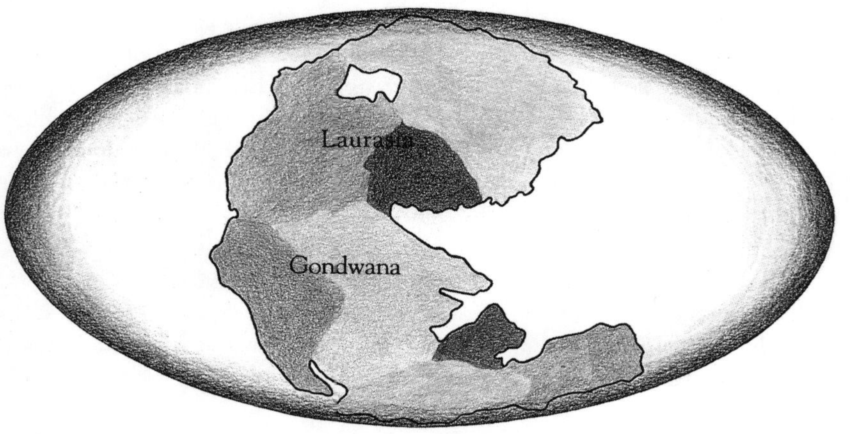


**The continents were still connected in the Jurassic Period.**

During the Cretaceous Period the continents gradually separated and moved north. At first the climate stayed damp and warm, but by the end of the Cretaceous Period (the Upper Cretaceous Period) it was becoming drier and the differences between summer and winter were developing. Volcanic eruptions formed mountains and thus the land area increased. Midway through the Cretaceous Period the vegetation began to change. Plants that we know today like deciduous trees and flowers started to grow. Dinosaurs could adjust to this new diet but not to the new climate.

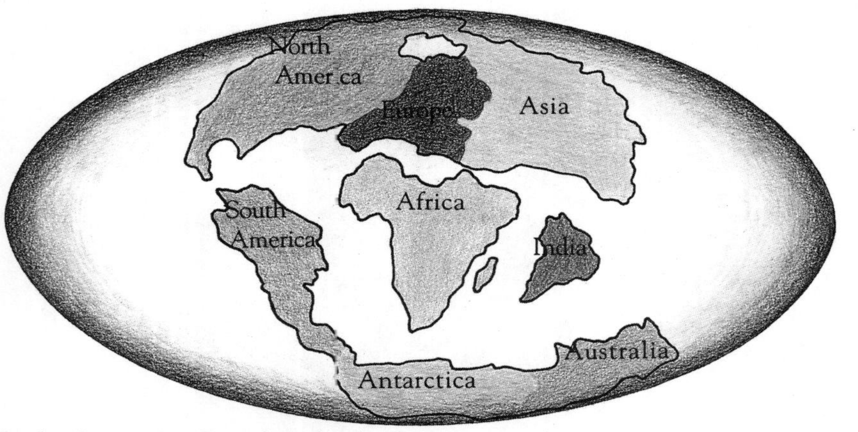


**During the Cretaceous Period the land masses separated.**

In the third picture you can see how similar the earth in the Upper Cretaceous Period was to our earth today. Compare this picture to a map of the world in an atlas. Today we too have a world made up of about one part land to two parts water. Most of the land mass lies north of the equator. Apart from that, we have four different seasons with different temperatures.

Now you know how the shape and the climate of the earth changed from the Mesozioc age to today. You are probably wondering how we can find plant and animal fossils and work out what they are when the earth has changed so much. The Alps, for example, were once covered by sea, so we can find the remains of ichthyosaurs, shells and squid there.

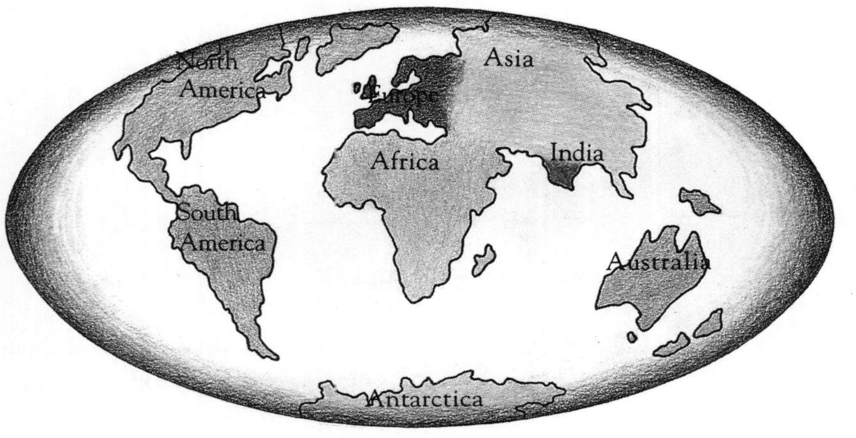


**This is what the earth looked like after the Upper Cretaceous Period. Compare it with an atlas and work out how the shape of the continents today has changed since then.**

| Paleozoic Age | | Mesozioc Age | | Cenozoic Age |
|---|---|---|---|---|
| 570 million years ago | 245 million years ago | 210 million years ago | 144 million years ago | 65 million years ago |

## Bone finds

An animal's dead body is called a cadaver or carrion. Usually it is eaten by scavengers and then further broken down by bacteria. The scavengers of the Mesozoic age include some small theropods (predatory dinosaurs), some pterosaurs, some mammals, and probably Tyrannosaurus rex too.

It can happen that a dead animal is quickly covered by sand or mud. In this case the cadaver does not completely decompose, and the teeth, bones, shell and the imprint of the body and footprints can remain and become fossilized over millions of years. So sometimes not just individual bones but whole skeletons of dinosaurs, ichthyosaurs and pterosaurs have been found. In some rare finds you can even see areas of skin.. This enables us to learn something about what their skin was like. The colour of the skin is one thing we don't know and have to guess at. Since dinosaurs are closely related to lizards and birds, which are often very brightly coloured, some scientists believe that dinosaurs were colourful, like parrots, or may have been able to change their colour for camouflage, like some lizards.

New skeletons are being found all the time and so scientists today are able to put together a much more exact picture of what dinosaurs looked like and how they lived. This also lets us learn more about how the earth and its other inhabitants developed. We can fit together bones by using modern animals' skeletons as models. In this way we can also complete skeletons with missing bones. Fossilized footprints teach us about an animal's posture, weight and even how fast it could run. All of this means that we can develop a very good picture of the dinosaur period. New finds of skeletons can verify hunches we have about dinosaurs or correct them. We now know, for example, that dinosaurs weren't sluggish, stupid, lazy creatures, but that their brain was in some cases as developed as those of modern birds.

Some dinosaurs cared for their young like mammals and birds. For some years now most scientists have believed that birds are descended from the smaller predatory dinosaurs.

Apart from birds, crocodiles and pterosaurs were close relatives of the dinosaur. Ichthyosaurs, snakes and lizards are more distant relatives.

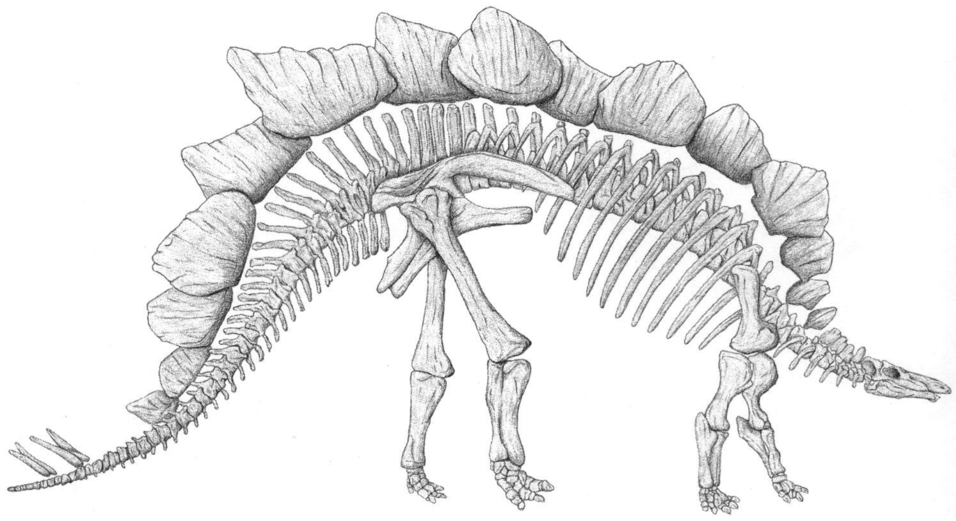

**This is a Stegosaurus skeleton. Use it to see whether you have put the puzzle together correctly.**

## What made them extinct?

Scientists have been asking this ever since research into dinosaurs began. Today there are two different theories. One theory is that a huge meteor hit the earth at the end of the Cretaceous Period, about 65 million years ago. The collision caused an increase in water and air temperature, which in turn caused poisonous gases to be produced. These gases blocked out the sun and as a result many plants and animals died.

But since not all of them died, some other scientists believe in another theory. They think that many volcanoes must have emerged during the formation of the mountains we know today, and that this changed the climate so much that animals like the dinosaur were no longer able to live on earth. Other species, such as most mammals, birds and crocodiles, found that they could develop further in this new world. One thing we do know is that the dinosaurs did not die out suddenly but gradually disappeared over a period of thousands of years.

# Dinosaurs

When dinosaurs developed, about 230 million years ago (at the end of the Triassic Period), they formed three groups. Two of these groups became herbivorous (eating vegetable matter only). They were the sauropods, such as Brachiosaurus (which means 'arm lizard'), and the ornithischians, such as Stegosaurus ('roofed lizard'). The third group were the carnivorous (meat-eating) theropods, such as Tyrannosaurus rex ('king of the tyrant lizards') or Velociraptor ('fast thief').

The sauropods became bigger and bigger (up to 40m) during the Jurassic Period, and their necks became longer and longer. This enabled them to reach food from the highest trees. Sauropods swallowed small stones in order to break up their food, just as geese and hens do today. The sauropods lived in herds and were able to use their powerful tails to defend themselves against predatory dinosaurs.

In comparison to the sauropods, the ornithischians were quite small. Many types became bigger over time, but they rarely grew to more than 10m. Some ran on two legs, some on four. The small ornithischians could easily run away from predatory dinosaurs. Some of the bigger species, such as Stegosaurus, developed bony plates or spikes to protect their bodies. Other animals like Euoplocephalus ('well armoured head') also had a bony club at the end of their tail with which to defend themselves. Yet others, like Lambeosaurus (named after its discoverer), had bony crests or bulges connected to the nose. This meant that their sense of smell was so developed that they could smell their enemy when it was still at some distance and flee. Bony head crests were hollow and their main function was for the amplification of sounds. Some ornithischians, like Triceratops ('three-horned face'), had horns and bony frills on the head which they used when fighting predatory dinosaurs.

Theropods always ran on two legs. Big animals like Tyrannosaurus rex or Ceratosaurus ('horned lizard') killed their prey with their teeth and their powerful jaws. The claws on their hands and feet became smaller over the course of their development. Small predators like Velociraptor killed their prey with the sharp claws on their hands and feet, and lived off mammals, lizards, eggs and carrion.

Here you can see animals from the three groups. At the top is the sauropodomorph Brachiosaurus, in the middle the ornithischian Lambeosaurus, and below the theropod Tyrannosaurus rex.

## Brachiosaurus

Brachiosaurus lived in the late Jurassic Period in what is now North America and Africa. Being 25m long and weighing in at about 40t it wasn't the longest dinosaur but it was the heaviest. It was over 12m tall and had a long neck and high shoulders. Brachiosaurus was the only dinosaur to have front legs longer than the back legs. It possibly had a trunk attached to its nose, which was located over the eyes.

Supersaurus was quite a close relative of Brachiosaurus. If you want to make a Supersaurus, then draw it taller and slimmer, as it was about 16m tall and 30m long.

You can make a Diplodocus ('double beam') by drawing it slimmer than Brachiosaurus and with a longer, more horizontal neck, shorter front legs and a very long tail. Diplodocus grew to about 27m long.

Brachiosaurus' relatives became smaller during the Cretaceous Period. You can make a Titanosaurus by drawing it half the size of Brachiosaurus and with bony plates at the hips. Scientists have found bony plates near Titanosaurus skeletons and can only presume that they were attached to the hips.

## Stegosaurus

Stegosaurus grew up to 9m long, weighed about 2t and ran on four legs. So far its skeletons have been found only in North America. Its spiky tail and the bony plates on its back protected it from enemies. These plates may also have influenced its body temperature since blood vessels ran through the skin that covered them. Stegosaurus and its relatives were unprotected on the sides (or flanks) of their bodies. It is noticeable that Stegosaurus had a small head and a small brain.

Relatives of Stegosaurus, including Kentrosaurus ('spiny lizard') from Africa and Dacentrurus ('spiny tail') from Europe can be made as follows: they were half the size of Stegosaurus. Instead of bony plates Dacentrurus had two rows of bony spikes and a spur on each hip. Kentrosaurus had bony plates and spikes. Brachiosaurus, Ceratosaurus, Allosaurus and Stegosaurus and their relatives all belong in the first landscape from the craft pages.

## Ceratosaurus

Ceratosaurus was a large theropod of the Jurassic Period. Its bones have been found only in North America and East Africa. Ceratosaurus was about 6m long, weighed about 600kg and ran, like all theropods, on two legs. Its enormous jaws contained fearsome teeth with which it killed its prey. The three horns on its skull are distinctive. There is one over each eye and another on the top of the nose. Unlike the later Tyrannosaurus rex, Ceratosaurus had long arms with four claws.

To make Allosaurus ('other lizard'), draw Ceratosaurus twice as big and replace the horn on its nose with a bulge reaching from between the eyes down to the snout. Draw three claws on the hands. Allosaurus also lived during the Jurassic Period.

## Triceratops

Triceratops was another member of the ornithischian order, the same order as Stegosaurus and Euoplocephalus. It lived in the Upper Cretaceous Period. So far bones have been found only in North America. Triceratops grew to 8m long, weighed nearly 5t and ran on four legs. Triceratops lived in herds and could defend itself well with its three horns. Its neck was protected from bites by a bony frill.

You will have to vary the number of horns and the type of bony frill to make Triceratops' relatives, which also lived in North America. Pentaceratops ('five-horned face') had five horns, two over the eyes, two on the cheeks and one on the nose. Centrosaurus ('lizard with a sharp spike') had one large horn and a short, rough bony collar. Styracosaurus ('spiky lizard') had a horn on the nose and a bony collar made up of six long serrated spikes. They were all about the same size as Triceratops.

Tyrannosaurus rex, together with Euoplocephalus, Triceratops and its relatives all belong in the second landscape from the craft pages.

## Tyrannosaurus rex

Tyrannosaurus rex lived at the end of the Cretaceous Period in North America. It was about 12m long, 5m tall and weighed about 7t. That is about the weight of a small loaded truck. But in spite of this Tyrannosaurus rex was able to move around quickly on two legs. Of course it was not as fast as, for example, Ceratosaurus. For that reason many scientists believe that it ate carrion. It used its sharp, approximately 15cm long teeth to tear up its prey. Unlike Ceratosaurus it had short arms with two weak claws on its hands.

You can easily make Tarbosaurus ('amazing lizard'), which was a close relative of Tyrannosaurus from Central Asia, by drawing it a bit smaller and slimmer.

You can make a South American relative of Tyrannosaurus by drawing the head somewhat smaller and adding horns to the top of the skull, like those of a buffalo. The body should be smaller than that of Tyrannosaurus. This new animal is Carnotaurus ('meat-eating bull').

## Euoplocephalus

Euoplocephalus ('armoured lizard') was an ankylosaur which lived during the Upper Cretaceous Period in North America. Euoplocephalus grew to about 7m long and 3t in weight and ran on four legs. It had a wide skull with many horns, a body covered in plates and spikes and a bony club at the end of its tail. Even its eyelids were protected with bone.

If you draw Euoplocephalus somewhat slimmer and with longer back legs then you will get Nodosaurus ('knotty lizard'). Omit the bony club on the tail, because scientists believe that the group of ankylosaur Nodosaurus belonged to did not have tail clubs.

## Velociraptor

Velociraptor, a small theropod, lived in the Upper Cretaceous Period. Its bones have been found in Central Asia. This dinosaur was barely 2m tall and weighed about 40kg. Like all theropods it ran on two legs. It killed its prey with the long sharp claws on its front and back feet.

Using Velociraptor as a model you can make two of its more distant relatives, Oviraptor ('egg thief') and Ornithomimus ('bird mimic'). These two small theropods had no teeth and probably lived on eggs, and on small animals. Oviraptor's head should be drawn shorter and with a horn on the nose. Ornithomimus' head should be a bit smaller and flatter, similar to an ostrich's head. Also, Ornithomimus' neck and tail were somewhat longer and slimmer than those of Velociraptor.

Oviraptor lived in what is now Central Asia, Ornithomimus in North America.

## Parasaurolophus

Parasaurolophus (which means 'lizard like Saurolophus') also lived in the Upper Cretaceous Period in North America. It was about 10m tall, 4t and ran on two legs.

A particularly distinctive feature of this animal is the long crest extending backwards from the back of the head. This crest was hollow and amplified the animal's calls just like a trombone. Since hadrosaurs had bony crests of various shapes you can imagine that they made various noises, just as a trumpet makes a different noise to a recorder.

It is easy to make Parasaurolophus' close relative Saurolophus ('crested lizard'), since it is the same size but its horn is only half the length.

Edmontosaurus, as well as Lambeosaurus, Saurolophus, Parasaurolophus and Velociraptor belong in the third landscape from the craft pages.

## Edmontosaurus

Edmontosaurus ('lizard from Edmonton') is a member of the hadrosaur group. They were given this name because their snouts are a similar shape to a duck's bill.

Edmontosaurus could grow up to 13m long, weighted 3t, ran on two legs and lived at the end of the Cretaceous Period in North America.

Like all hadrosaurs, it had very strong jaws with about 2,000 teeth to grind up vegetable matter. Once teeth had worn down, new ones grew to replace them.

By drawing Edmontosaurus somewhat smaller you will get Hadrosaurus. Its nostrils were located in a round bulge. Hadrosaurus was about 8m long and also lived in North America. The hadrosaur group is named after it.

## Lambeosaurus

Lambeosaurus was one of the biggest hadrosaurs and grew up to 9m long and about 2t and ran on two legs. It lived in the Upper Cretaceous Period and so far its bones have been found only in North America.

Like many hadrosaurs, Lambeosaurus had a bony crest on the head, shaped differently on males and females. The male, illustrated below, had a horn projecting backwards from the end of the crest.

To make a female, omit the horn and make the bony crest smaller.

You could also make Tsintaosaurus ('lizard from Qingdao'). It was almost as big as Lambeosaurus and had a broader snout. Tsintaosaurus had a more pointed horn at the back of the head and lived in China.

## A dinosaur quiz

**1. Were there humans living at the same time as dinosaurs?**

**2. What are the dinosaur's closest relatives?**

**3. When did the dinosaurs live?**

**4. What was the climate like at the time of the dinosaurs?**

**5. Were all dinosaurs giants?**

**6 What is the difference between a reptile and a mammal?**

If you read the information pages carefully then you will easily be able to find the correct answers. Get someone to help you.

Perhaps you and your friends or parents could make up new quiz questions.

---



First published in Great Britain by
**The Lutterworth Press**
**P.O. Box 60**
**Cambridge CB1 2NT**

**British Library Cataloguing-in-Publication Data.**
A catalogue record for this book is available from the British Library.

ISBN 0-7188-2851-8



Cover picture: Michael Zorn, Wiesbaden
Drawings: Bernd Burkart, Stuttgart
Information pages: Wilhelm Knobloch; page 2 (A word about paper and Dinosaur game): Jutta Schmidt-Rettig.
English text: translated by Penelope Griffin
Consultant: Dr Angela Milner, British Museum (Natural History), London

Printing: SVA, Ludwigsburg

Brachiosaurus